METAMORPHOSES

METAMORPHOSES

Poetry: Sheryl St. Germain
Artwork: Janet Morgan

An Art & Adventures Publication

Some of these poems have appeared in the following journals and anthologies: *Louisiana Literature, Sands, The Prose Poem, Blaze* and *Epiphanies: The Prose Poem Now.*

Grateful acknowledgement is extended to The Texas Institute of Letters and The University of Texas at Austin, co-sponsors of the Dobie-Paisano Fellowship, which provided the author time to work on some of these poems.

Contact:
Sheryl St. Germain
208 S. Millvale Avenue
Pittsburgh, PA 15224
sstgermain@chatham.edu
412-661-1809
Poetry and Art

Janet Morgan
www.Janetmorgan-art.net
art@janetmorgan.net

By the sea or before a mountain, lost among the trees of a forest or at the entrance to a valley that spreads out at our feet, our first sensation is strangeness or separation. We feel different. The natural world presents itself as something alien, possessing an existence of its own. This estrangement soon turns into hostility. Each branch of the tree speaks a language we do not understand; from each thicket a pair of eyes spies on us; unknown creatures threaten or mock us. And the opposite may occur: nature turns inward and the sea heaves and plunges before us, indifferently; the rocks become even more dense and impenetrable; the desert, more vacuous and inaccessible. We are nothing in relation to so much existence turned in on itself. And from this feeling that we are nothing we proceed, if contemplation is prolonged and panic does not overtake us, to the opposite state: the rhythm of the sea keeps time with that of our blood; the silence of the rocks is our own silence; to walk among the sands is to walk through the span of our consciousness, as boundless as they; the forest murmurs allude to us. We are part of all. Being emerges from nothing. The same rhythm moves us, the same silence surrounds us.

—Octavio Paz
Tr. Ruth L.C. Simms

Table of Contents

Introduction

Ovid writes, in his own book of *Metamorphoses,* that after Daphne's arms became branches and her feet rooted and held, Apollo could still hear her heart beating underneath the bark. This mythic metamorphosis always fascinated me because of its incompleteness: Daphne retains some of her human qualities, not unlike Gregor, Kafka's infamous protagonist in a much later metamorphosis. A woman turned in a tree, a man turned into a bug (or, for that matter, a fly), a woman turned into a cow—this is the stuff of myth, fantasy, science fiction, interesting precisely because the transformations are imperfect. Daphne, in Ovid's version of her myth, never becomes, completely, "tree," or "other." She remains suspended, a female heart within a tree, with only a memory of human speech, of what it was to be human.

Pablo Neruda's well-known poem on the art of writing poetry, "Ars Poetica," begins "Entre sombra y espacio," which has been translated in English at least twelve different ways, including "between shadow and space" and "between dark and the void." What is most important about that line, though, is *the act of being between.* The moment before writing the poem is a moment, for Neruda, of being able to live in between two things, to be both oneself and another. In the state of connection between self and other, whether that other be some aspect of the physical world or another human, lies a land full of possible insights and wisdoms.

It is a kind of twilight state, neither one nor the other, but somehow both.

I like very much the French expression for twilight, *entre chien et loup* (between dog and wolf), because it articulates vividly the nature of that place that can only be defined by saying it is the state of being between. This state is a particularly potent one for the artist and writer who usually try to articulate human ambivalence and possibility. This state of being oneself *and* the other, this state of being *entre chien et loup*, is a kind of partial metamorphosis, a state in which an understanding of the self and the other can arise that would have been impossible if one had not been able to *imagine* being the other. In this book Janet Morgan and I have focused on woman and the natural world as self and other, but as a model, the imaginative act of (incomplete) metamorphosis has broader implications.

Some years ago I was doing research on contemporary French women poets, when I came across a poem by the poet Annie Salager entitled "La Femme-Buisson" ("The Woman-Bush"). The poem was written from the point of view of a woman who had turned into a bush, but she was also very much a woman; it put me in mind, of course, of the Daphne-Apollo myth. The problems I faced in translating the poem were both frustrating and fascinating, and led me, finally, to begin writing the poems in this book. "La Femme-Buisson" is heady, sensuous and musical. As a translator I could not compromise on the music, since the woman-bush had no language but music—the sounds of leaves, the wind, the insects inside the branches. Nor did I feel I could compromise on the other qualities of the poem. It seemed each word in the original had been chosen for its precise indication with respect to music, concept and sensuousness. I nearly went crazy with the translation—it obsessed me, like another you can never quite know. It seemed to me I had to become the poem in order to translate it. I began climbing trees, I had a photographer friend take a photograph of me inside a bush and print it in such a way that it seemed the bush and the image of the woman were one. I meditated on the photograph, I read and re-read the Daphne-Apollo myth.

Eventually I "finished" and published the translation, but I can hardly bear to read it, for I, more than anyone else, know what is not there. It was, of course, impossible to recreate the original with the kind of meticulousness I had envisioned; the translation, the metamorphosis from one language to another, remained incomplete for me.

What I learned about translation is that it is almost always a kind of partial metamorphosis, frustrating because it is never complete. The translation can never *be* the original, just as the beloved can never be us, although we may believe that that union is the object.

Though my inability to render Salager's poem into English left me frustrated, it also left me inspired. Her attempt to unite the voice of a woman and that of a bush continued to haunt me. I began writing my own poems from the point of view of a woman who had been transformed into a tree, which then broadened into poems in which other aspects of the physical world "spoke" as women. The poems included in this book, inspired by "La Femme-Buissson," are surreal meditations on the physical world, imagining, as Ovid did, that there was, figuratively, a woman's heart beating there.

I hoped these meditations would lead to some insight with respect to the human condition. Some of them were begun several years ago as war with Iraq began to seem inevitable and I, paralyzed with the implications of war, and daily ever more horrified, found I could not write in the direct, colloquial voice I had found so comfortable for so many years. I do not know where the voices in these poems have come from; I do know that they feed ancient and as real to me as a vivid dream or nightmare.

The poems seemed to want to be prose poems—that's how they came out, though in retrospect, the prose poem is the least "fixed" poetic form, defined by its being precisely between prose and poetry, thus appropriate for what I was trying to do.

I had written less than half the poems included in this book when I decided to contact the artist Janet Morgan. We had worked together on a previous book, *The Mask of Medusa*, and she had done the cover for another chapbook of poems for me, *Going Home*. I knew she was working on a series of goddess portraits; that she was interested in the nature of women and myth; that we were on the same wavelength. I knew I could send her fragments, ideas, even words that she could work from, and I knew that I could work from her own pieces, which had inspired me in the past.

In some cases I sent only one word to Janet, and I worked the poem from the drawing she sent. Sometimes I sent more—an idea for a poem, sometimes a rough draft, less often a finished poem. Sometimes she sent me drawing that connected with no poem I had yet written, but were somehow in the spirit of what we were doing, and I wrote a companion poem. The goal was not to redo in words or in drawings, what the other had done, not to *become* the other, but to be connected with the other in some deep way, to be in conversation with the other. The drawings in this book are not intended as illustrations of the poem, nor are the poems intended to explain the drawings. Although there are connections between the two—maybe an image, or a kind of starkness or richness, or a feeling; the two are, rather, companions, translations, indeed, one might even call them metamorphoses of each other.

We have not included my translation of the Salager poem, but rather my adaptation of the poem. Although its title, "Woman-Bush," is a literal translation of Salager's title, my poem is an imitation, a salute and celebration of the poem I failed to translate. As is this book.

—Sheryl St. Germain, Pittsburgh 2020

I. WATER

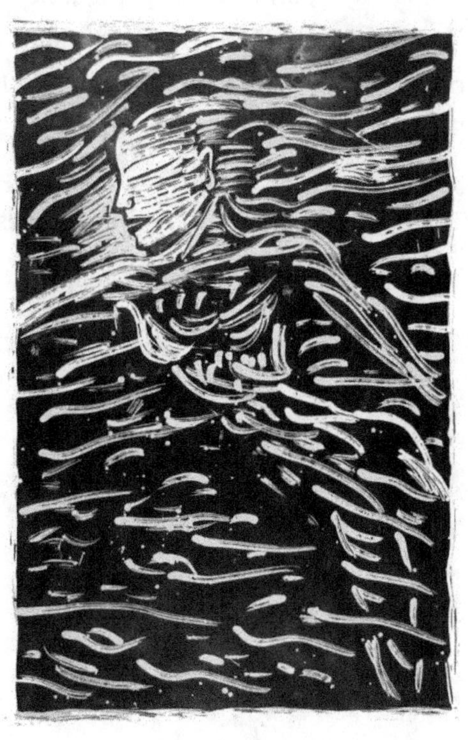

BAYOU

She is many, and the long fingers of her waters reach deep
into the south. Houses with families are born in the cradles
of her hips. Their men ride her skin looking for food.
Back in their houses, women invoke her, salt, spice her.

The aroma of their edible bayous fills the air.

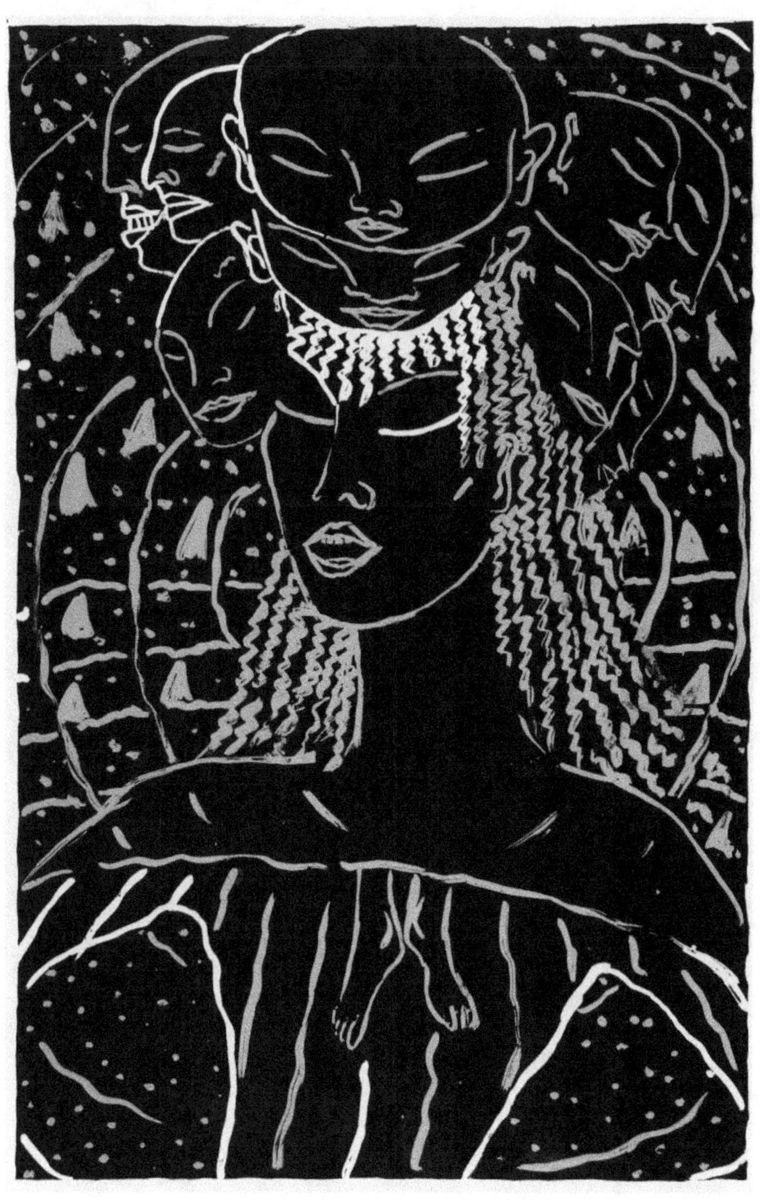

RIVER

She holds the city in the crook of her arm long past its childhood. She challenges the sun, sending its brilliance back mirrored with hers. The moon she welcomes, and together they lap at lovers who embrace at their edges. In old age she calls women too desperate for life. Tomorrow she will begin again with the sun, the lovers, birth, death.

She alone knows our muddy history, she alone is constant in her movement. My heart stops and I see myself in her brown waters. I want to speak, but I do not know her tongue.

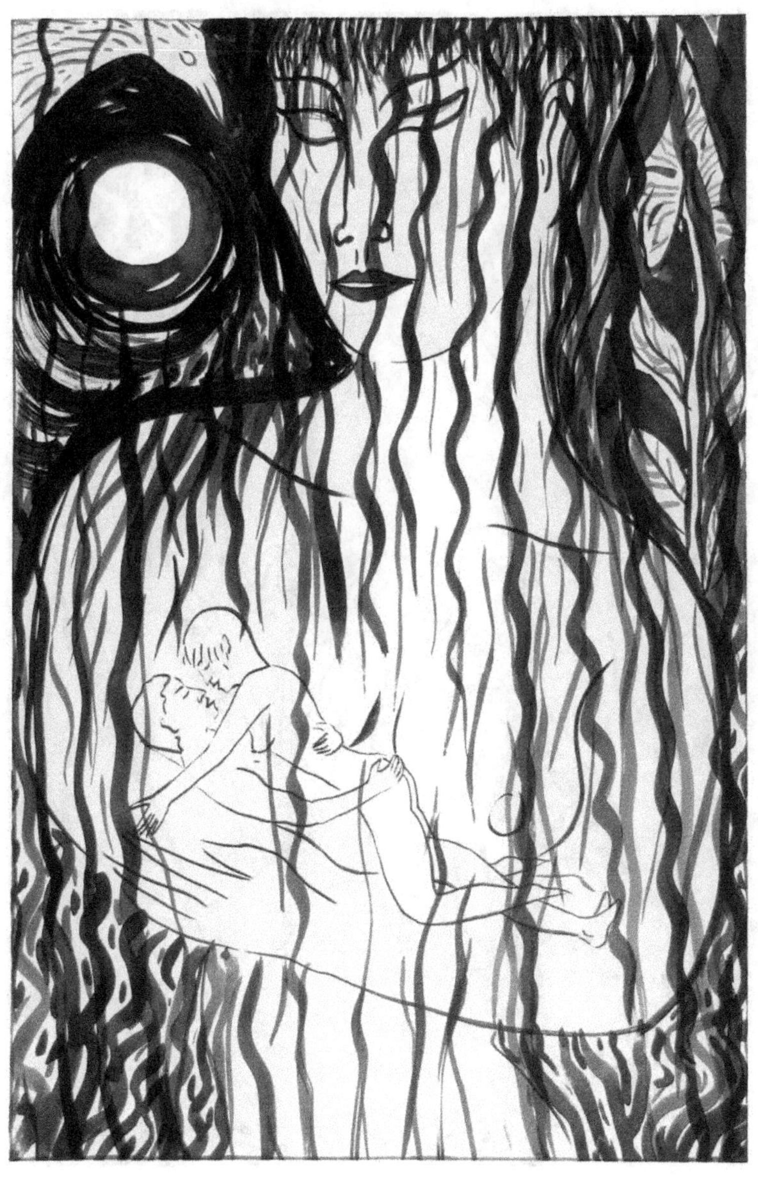

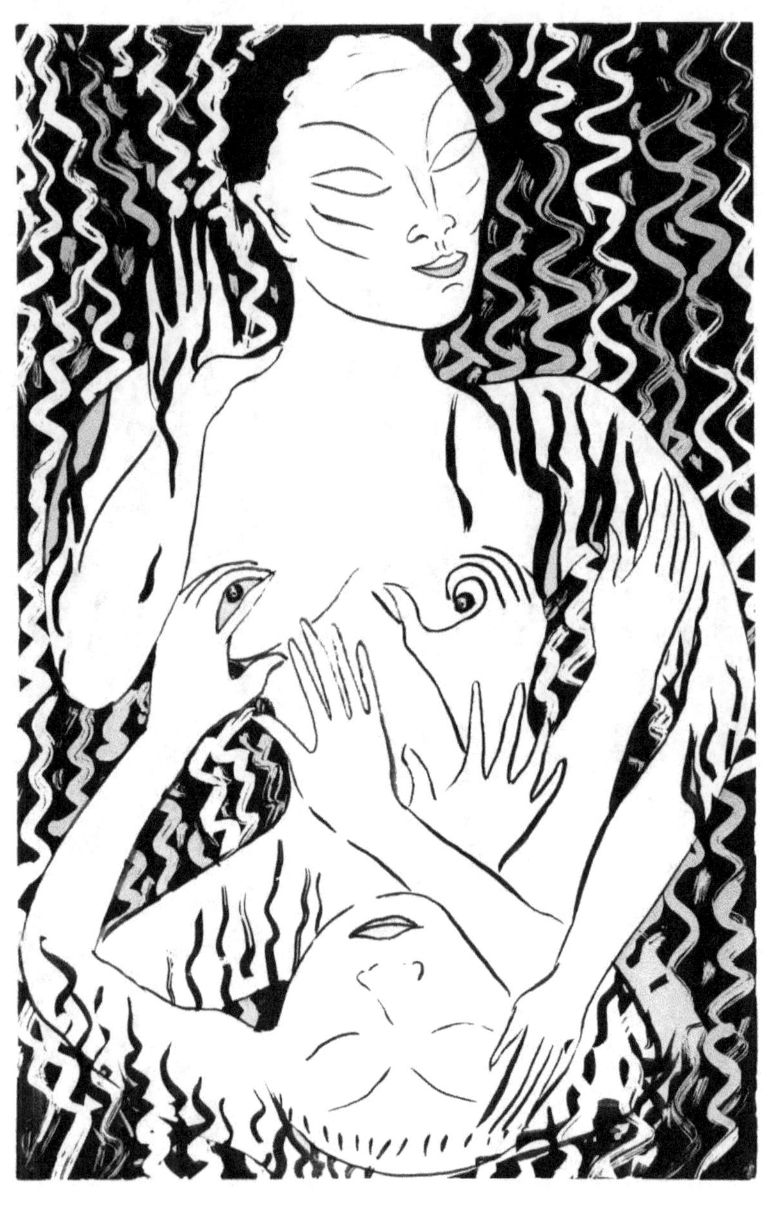

LAKE

As I lie back to back with the water I hear the lake shivering, slipping in and out of my ear like a lover's tongue. The night is a breath heavy with pine and flower and mist. It presses me down on the water, and the deeper muscles of the lake offer me up again. I float like this, caught between night and water, for hours.

The water seeps through pores of skin filling the spaces between fingers and toes sliding rushing cool between lips and legs when you open and press lifting and licking the hair on head underneath arms splitting into puzzles of creeks that twist through forests of hair. If you lie still enough, the water becomes animal, swirls around, lifts your breasts high, presses its mouth on your nipples until they feel like diamonds, until they cut the water's skin and stare with your eyes into night.

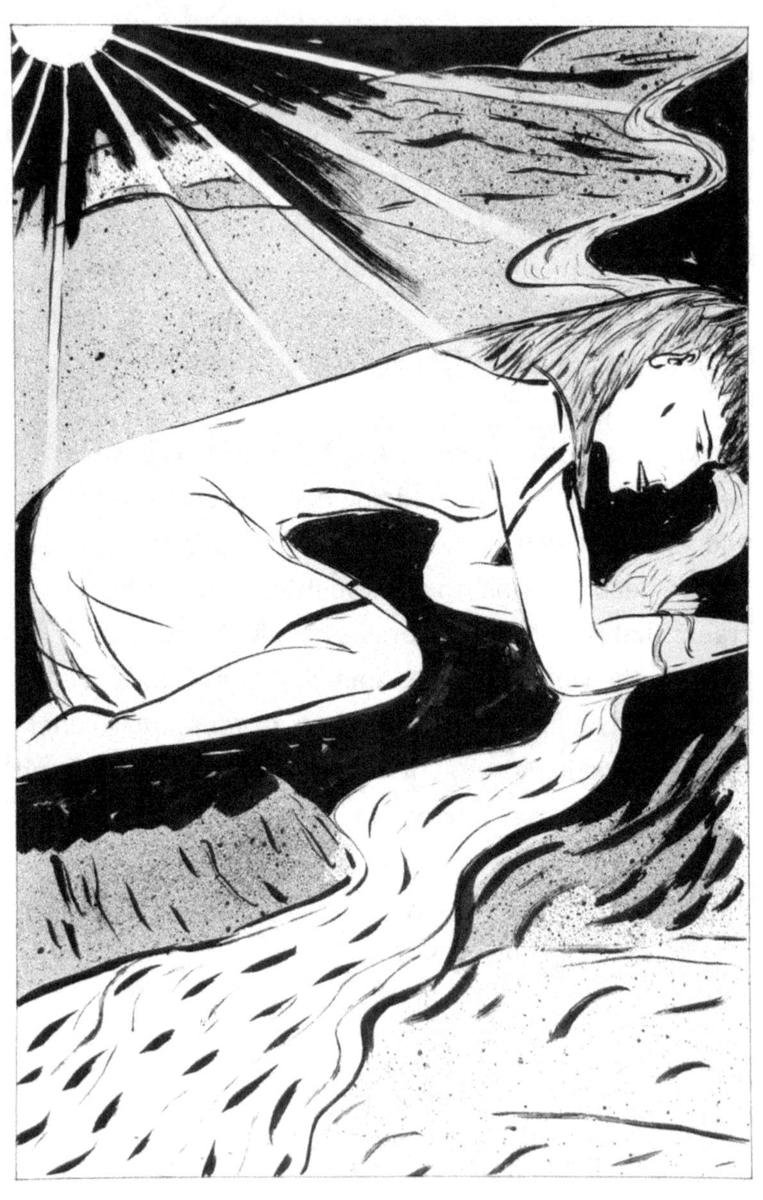

CREEK

She winds and rises, thins to shell where there is no love, fattens where the bed becomes generous, makes her children there. Her beauty is small, unlike a river's, though she is fat with fish and swells in spring, floods, breathes, mutters through rock, violently whispering a path that is always changing, always the same.

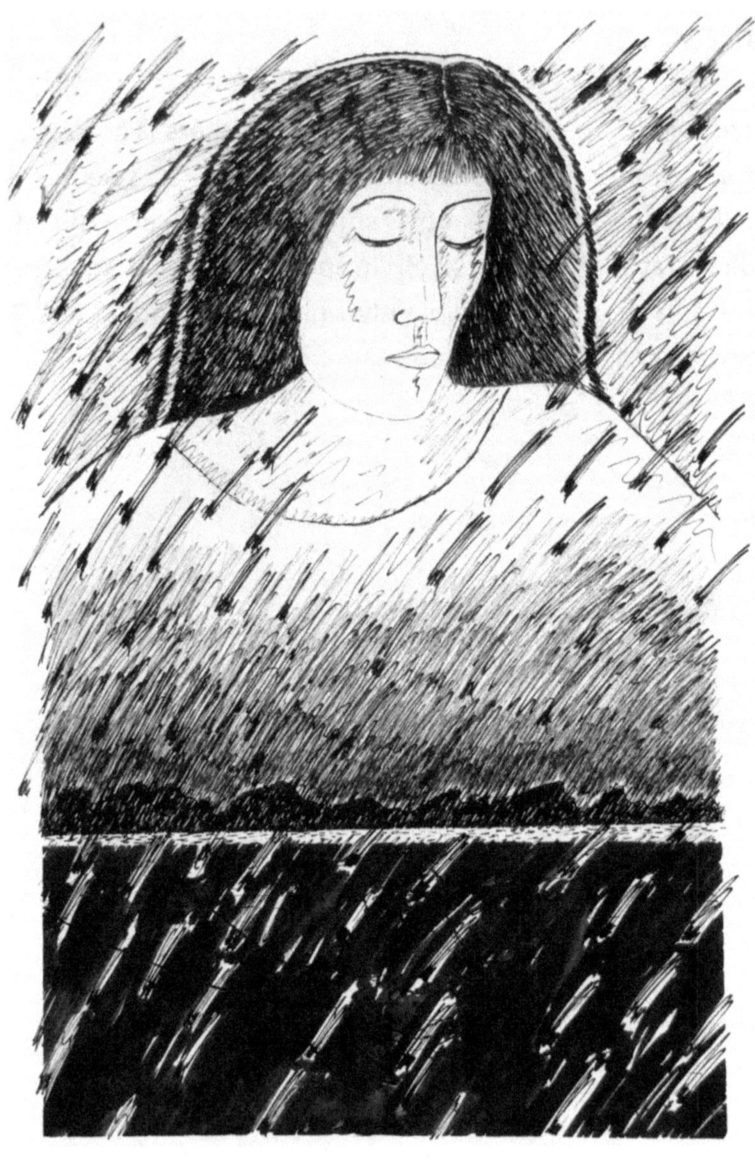

RAIN

When I am cloud, I am nothing.

When I split and become myself, it is not weeping, but multiplying myself into the grasses, down to your mouths.

When I have gone from cloud to this, I am strong.

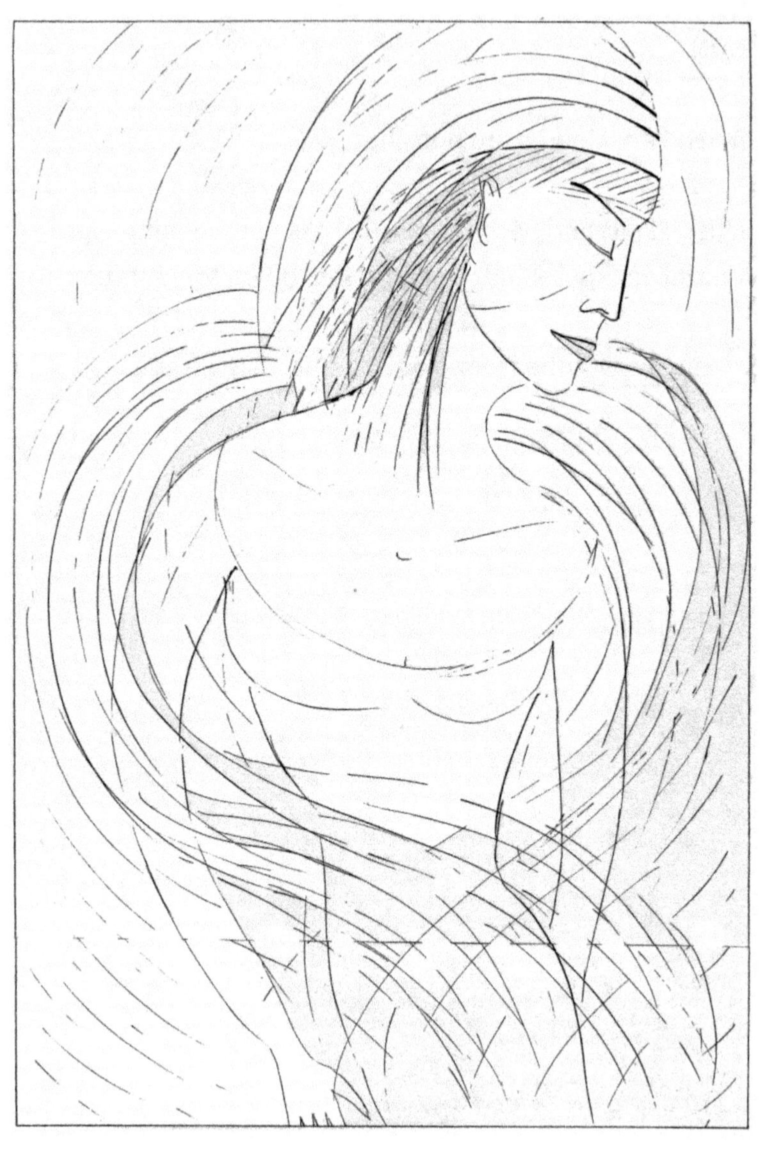

FOG WOMAN

I am the one who calls the fish, I have only to dip my hands
in the water and they come, the delicious salmon you love.
Day after day I bring you fish I bring you my love, my fishy,
delicious love, and I remain visible for you, my love, my
breasts here to touch, my mouth to kiss.

But beat me once my hard Raven, speak rough and brag of
the salmon as if you had caught them and I will disappear
to fog--water and air, no mouth, no breast no fish no kiss.

II. Earth

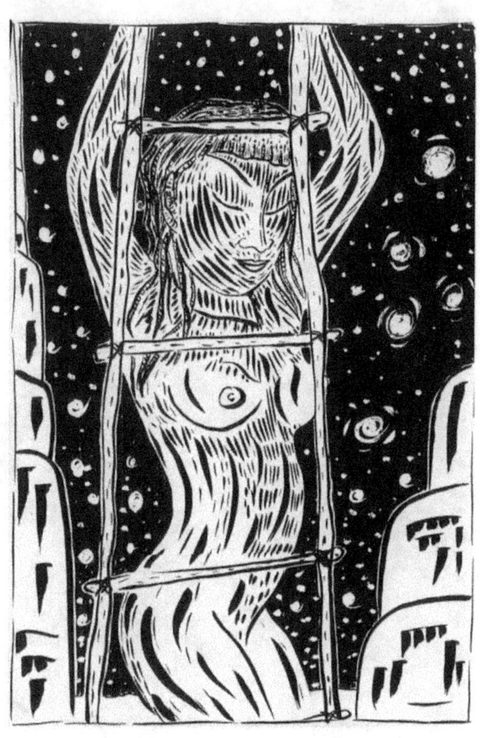

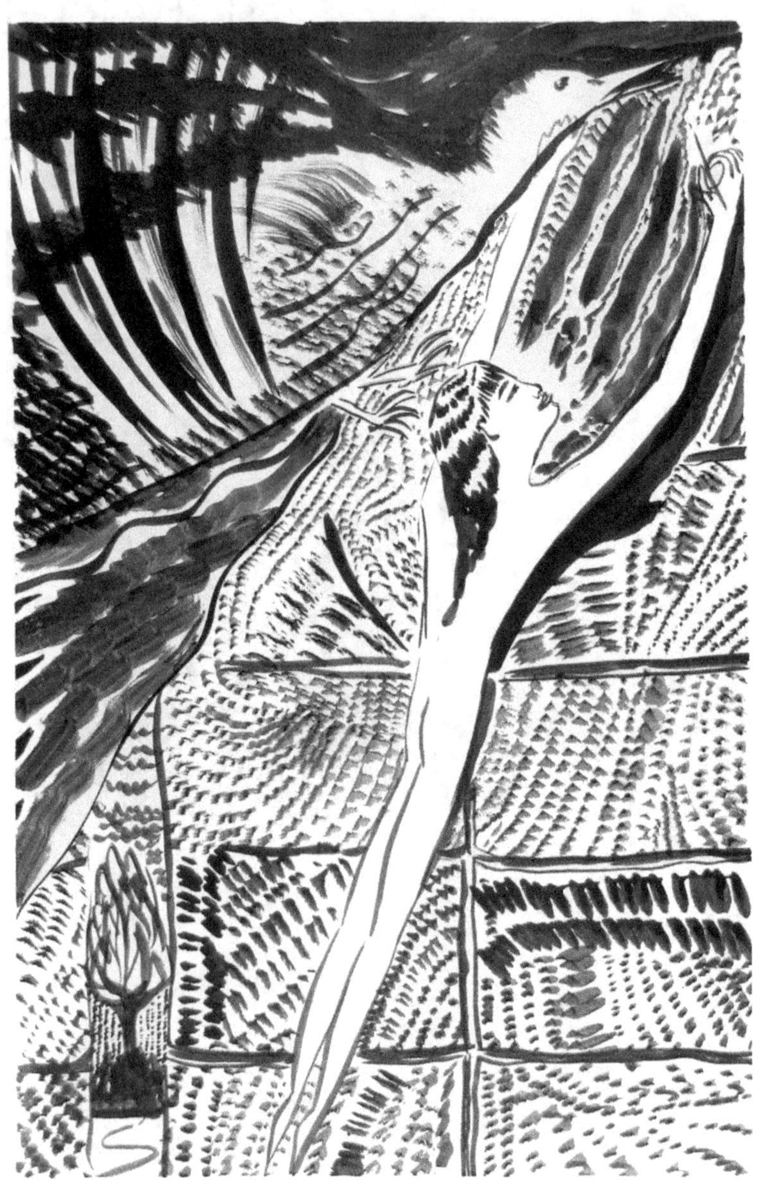

BLUFFS

I do not live on the bluffs, I *am* the bluffs, I am what is left
where waters of rivers spoke for thousands of my years.

I have become tall by waiting. To see me is to be taken
into me as one beloved, to be held against what is
destroyed in me.

I bare my naked, cut side to sun.

DESERT

I am dunes with their geometric hips and thighs, I am black sand that has allowed the wind to shape it, I am roots of mesquite that reach deeper than sanity would say for water.

Lie naked on my sands and I will make fire on your tongue.

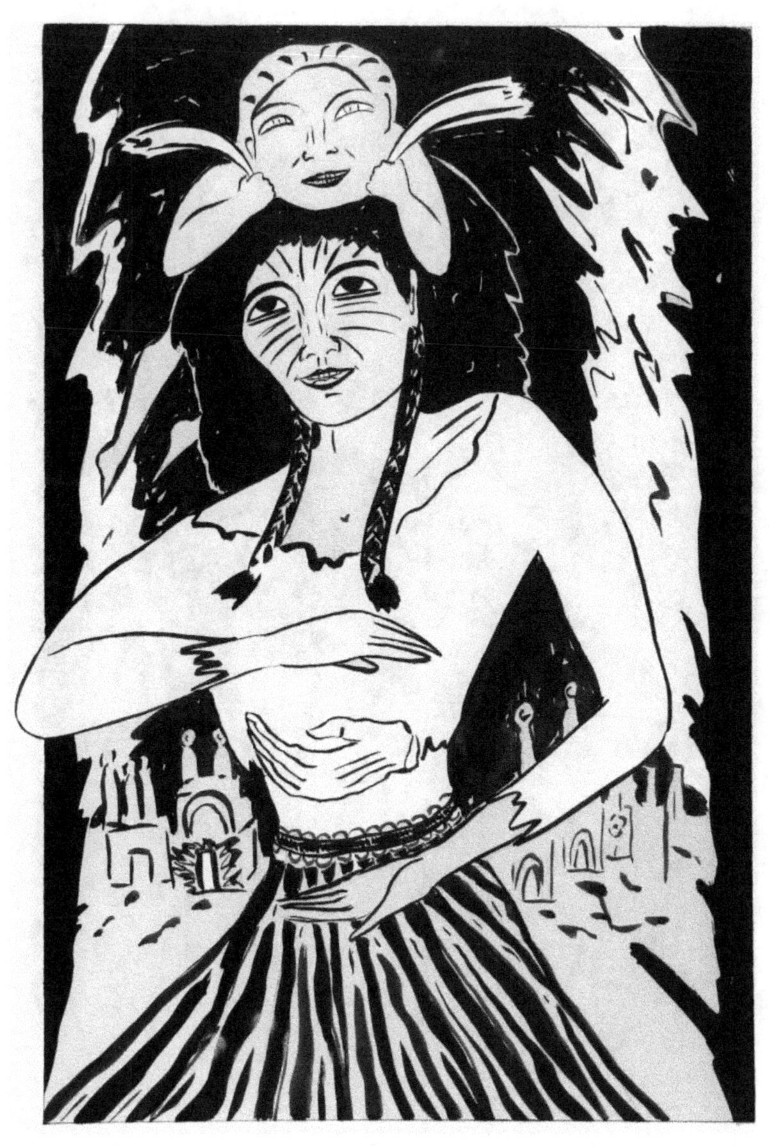

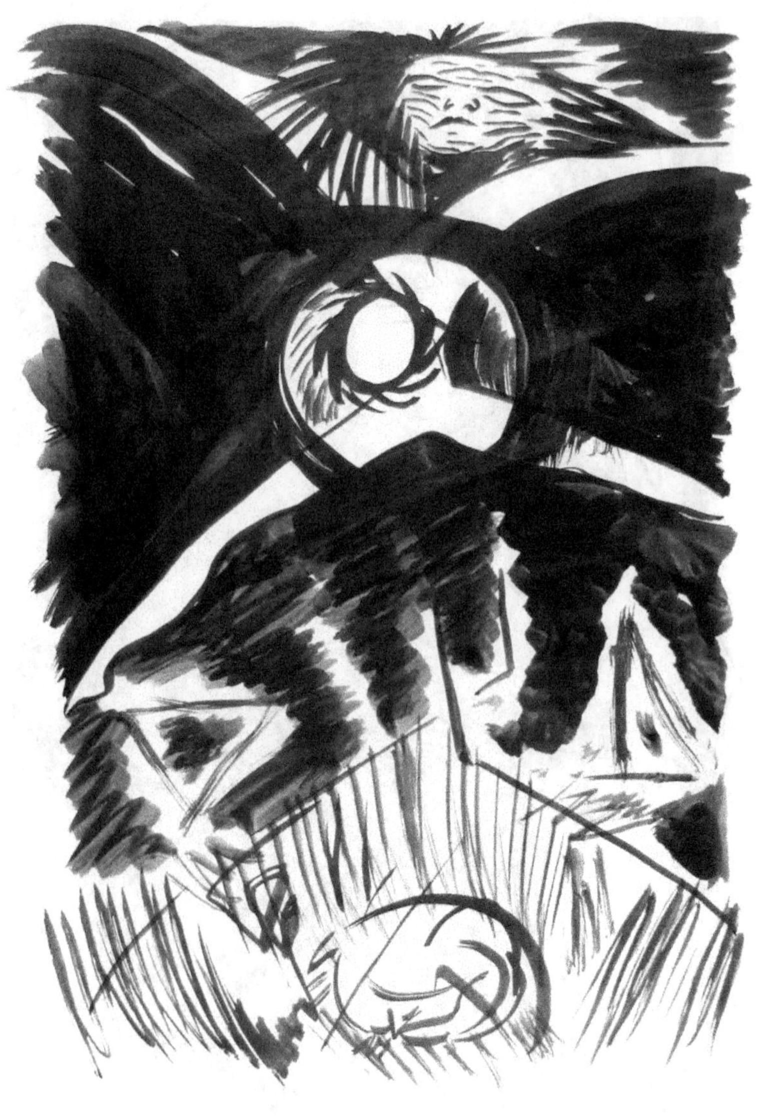

MUD

I am what you cannot forget, like a cancer I return with rain, I turn again to blood. I am always underneath you, loving you or sucking at you.

You don't see me because you don't look down.

I, on the other hand, have nothing to do but look.

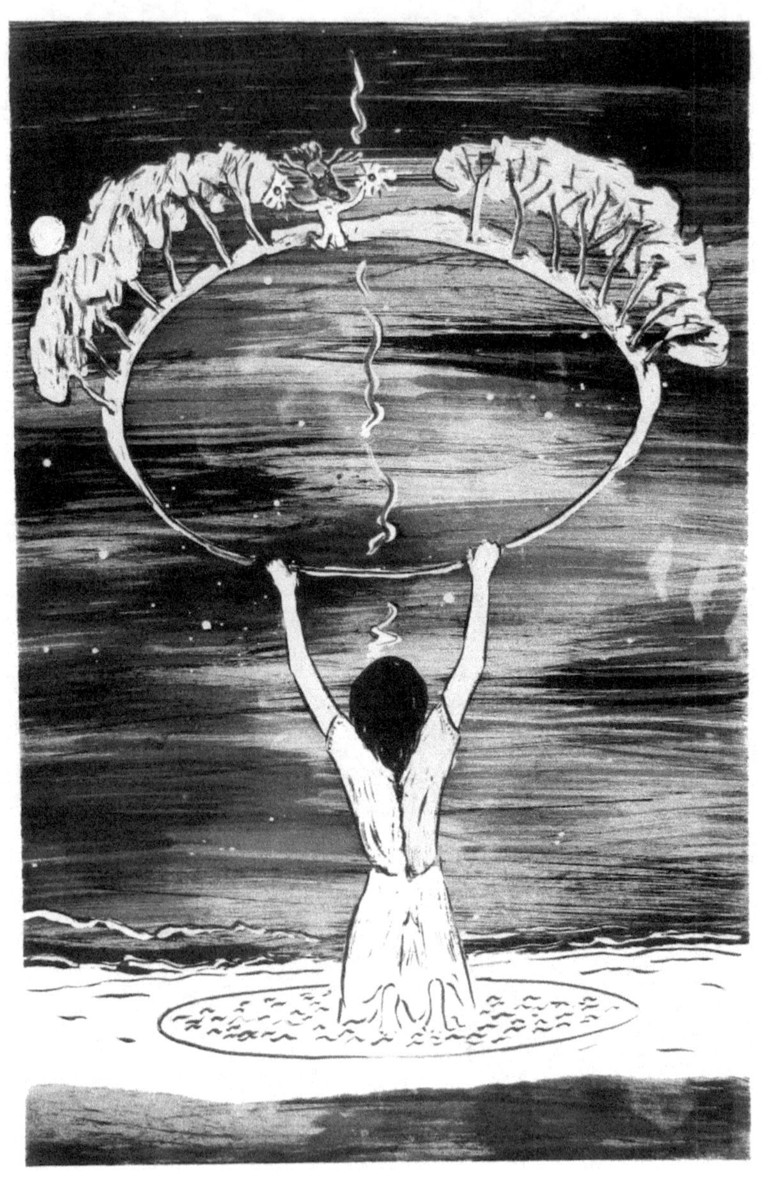

ROCK

You will all become her, finally.

Death, to know what she knows: stillness of heart and breath, dark joy of time unending, where there is no language.

Stone, where all is love, all is finally other.

STAR

My sister is rock. I am her bright twin still with language. I speak for her darkness though my words are already dead when I speak them. I am admired because I have a language she does not, because she is close and I am far.

But I tell you: we are one, and I will be happiest when this outer glowing fades, this false language that can never say what I mean, can never speak of death, and the inner silence, hotter and more beautiful than what I have now.

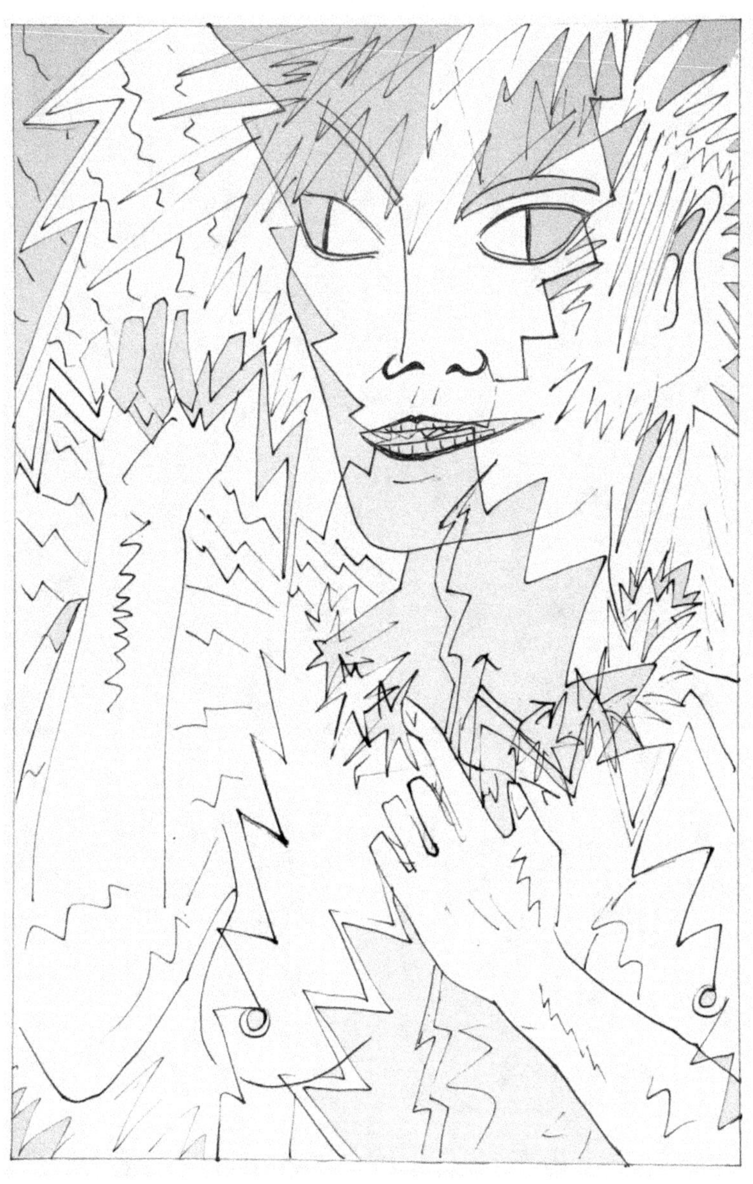

III. Air and Fire

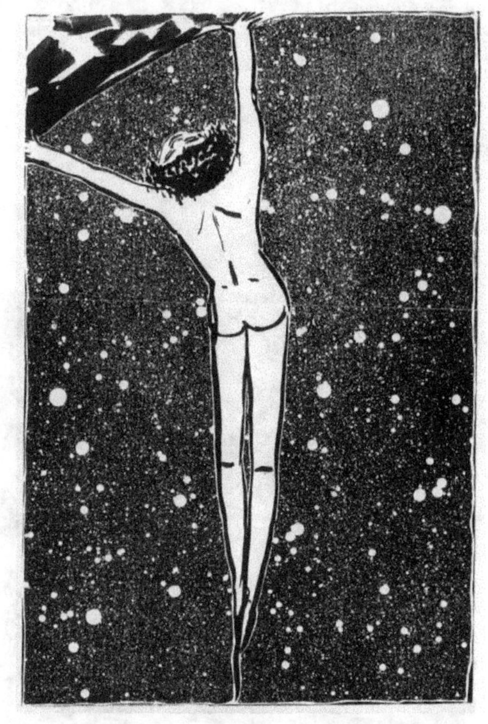

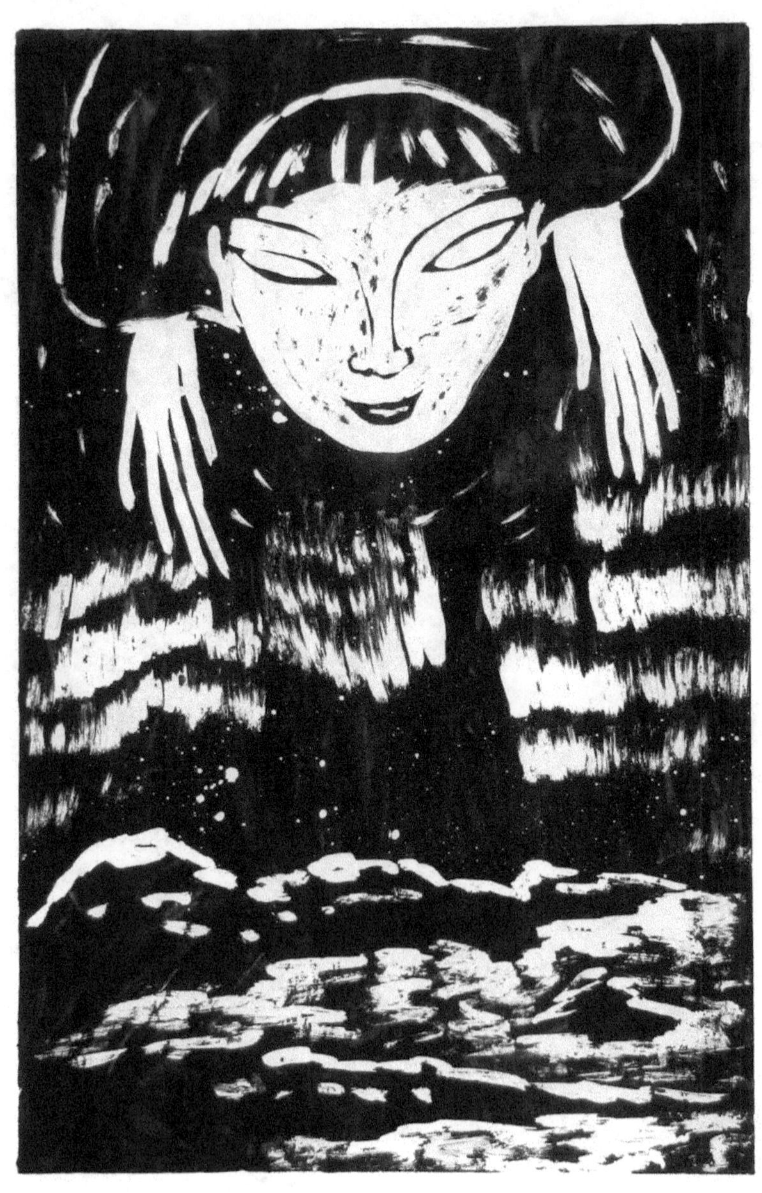

SKY

On this horizon shells of clouds shiver and whiten into themselves. Broken faces lace together with blue threads of sky, then thin into patterned veils searching for new mouths of air.

On the other horizon darker clouds blacken and rumble into arms, legs, and thighs bathing in the sting of electric lightning. Black turns slowly to purple; purple reddens into an open wound the whole sky long.

In one fierce moment the clouds give up all their moisture, raining thick glass-slivers of sea. A new gray tenses itself along the curve of the world.

If someone swung an ax through it, this sky would bleed.

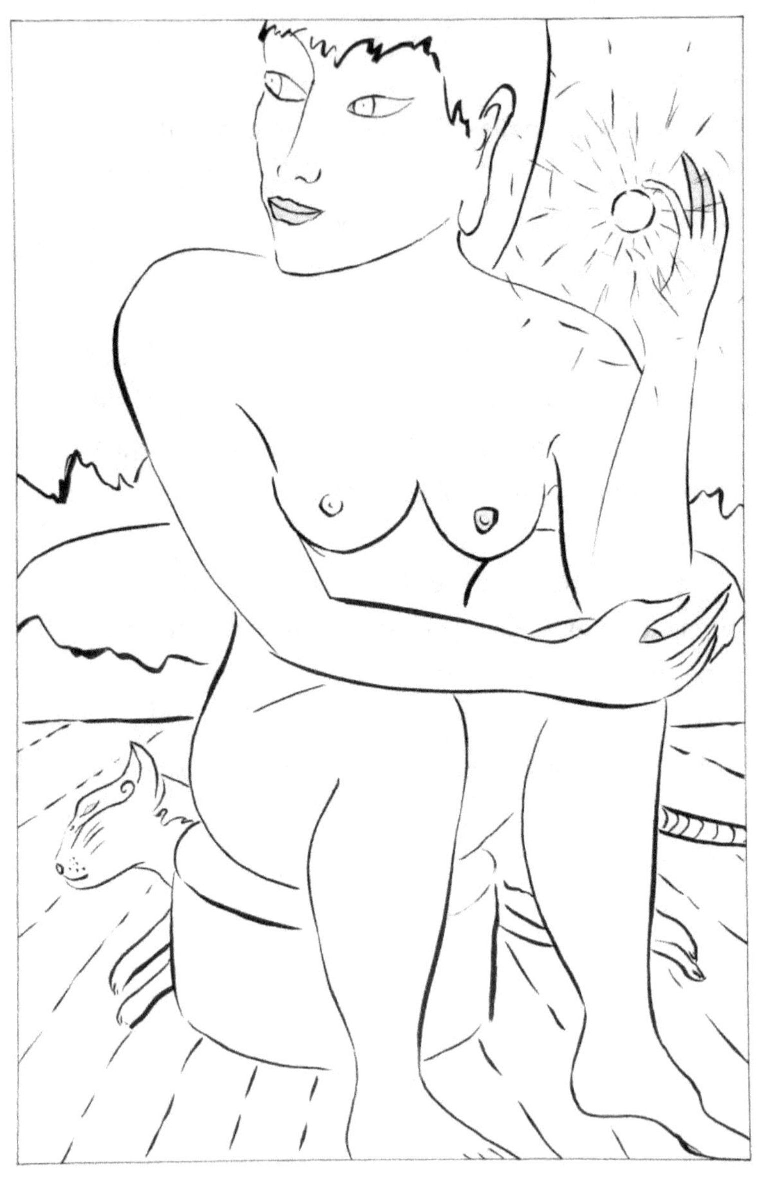

SUN

—in memory, Edith Södergran

I want to touch my hands to her milk white skin, to breathe in the sweet sun of her hair, to see earth with her large gray eyes. It is not the light of Apollo that lives in her, but the slow burning coals of mothers.

She was my age when she died, she fed on her words, coughed them up with her blood. She once wrote that the sun filled her breasts with honey, but I say that she is the sun. She, who is Enheduanna, she who is Sappho, she who is Emily, Edith. *Dress us, burn us, woman, poet, sun.*

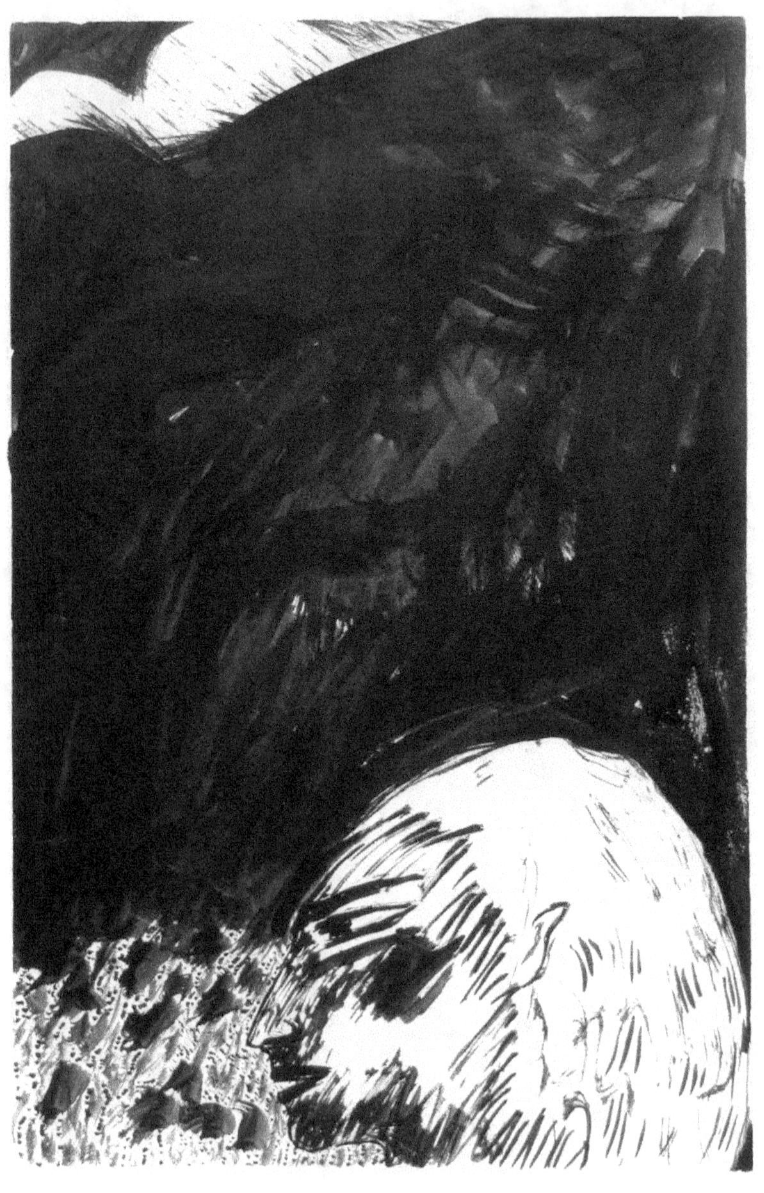

NIGHT

When sun is leached from the sky and even the moon can bear to give no light, birds lose their voices. Insects become hoarse, and night throws a muffler around its own throat.

The ancient tree outside my window shivers. Doors lock themselves and those with evil purpose position themselves behind shrubs.

Darkness comes only at night. Or else we do not hear the slow clenching of fist, the low bruise of voices when sun cries noon and rises full-blooded in us.

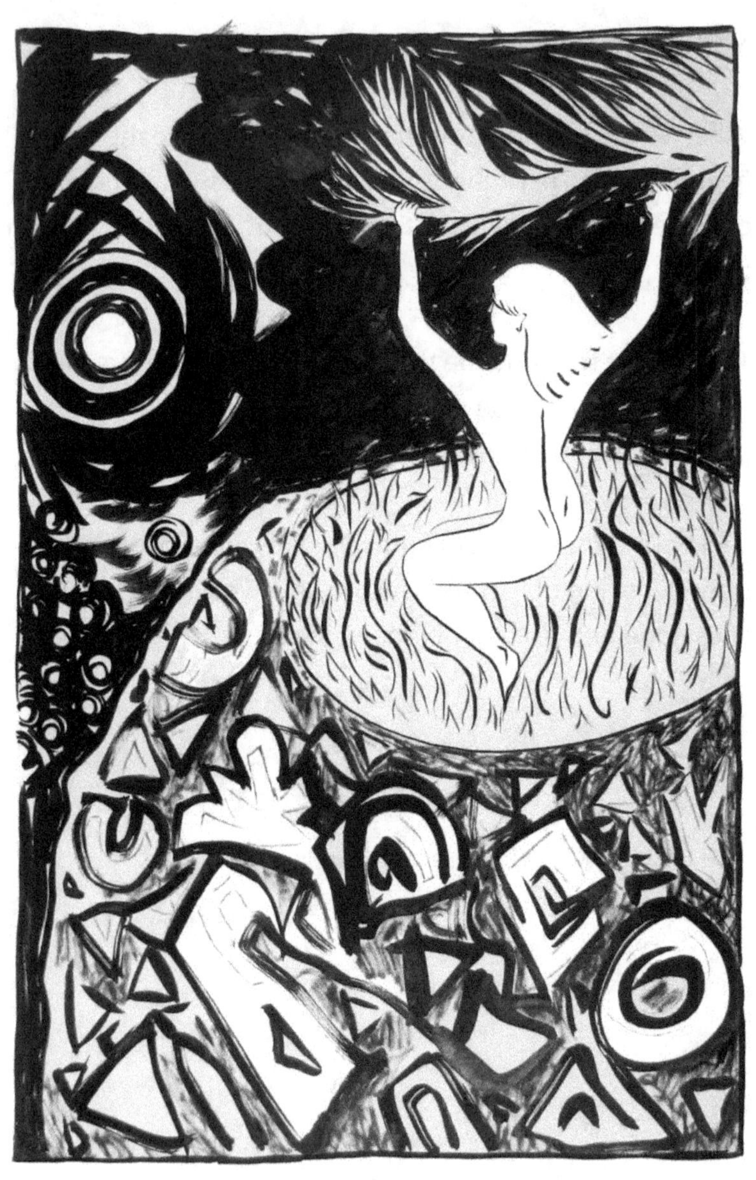

FIRE

I am music, vowels, desire, I am burning of all the dead words, all the paralyzed sentences. I am singing, I am green, all the seeds waiting for my heat to burst them, to make them become something rooted.

I am water, crackling raindrops, liquid flames.

Forget all that you know.

IV. Vegetable

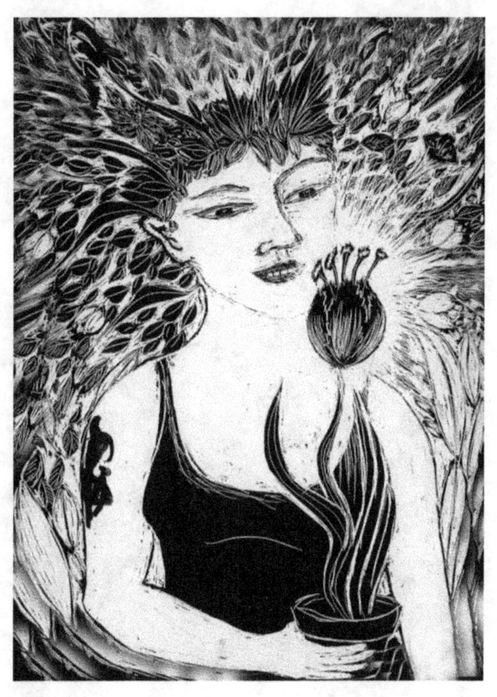

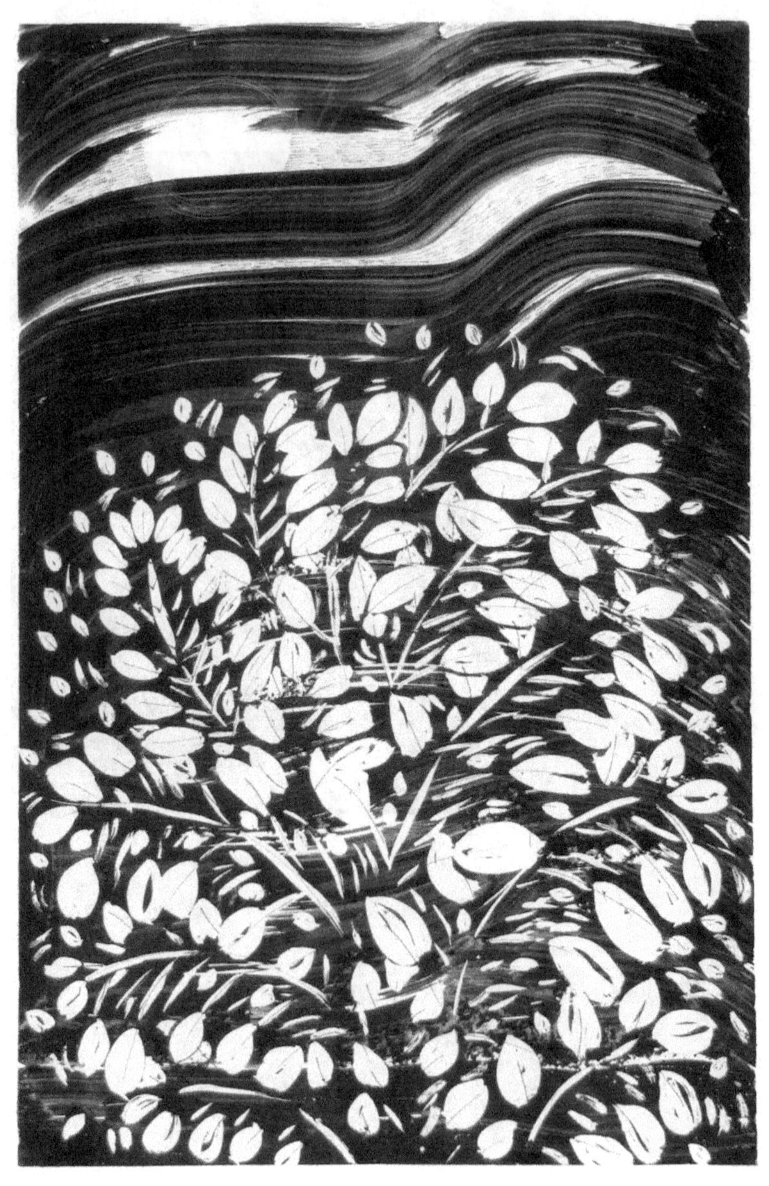

WOMAN-BUSH

My leaves whisper in the moon-washed air, a small breathing into a larger silence. Almost a voice, almost a moan into the night that prolongs it, holds it. The wind erases my voice as it collects it, as if it were the cry of some animal, the wind is a flue for the green smoke of my speech, a speech no one recognizes as speech, not human speech.

There are no words here, no words to reach me, to unknot me from this life, only the music of the night, the music of what I have become, its dark flooding harmonies, its hearts deep within my bark.

—After Annie Salager's "La Femme-Buisson"

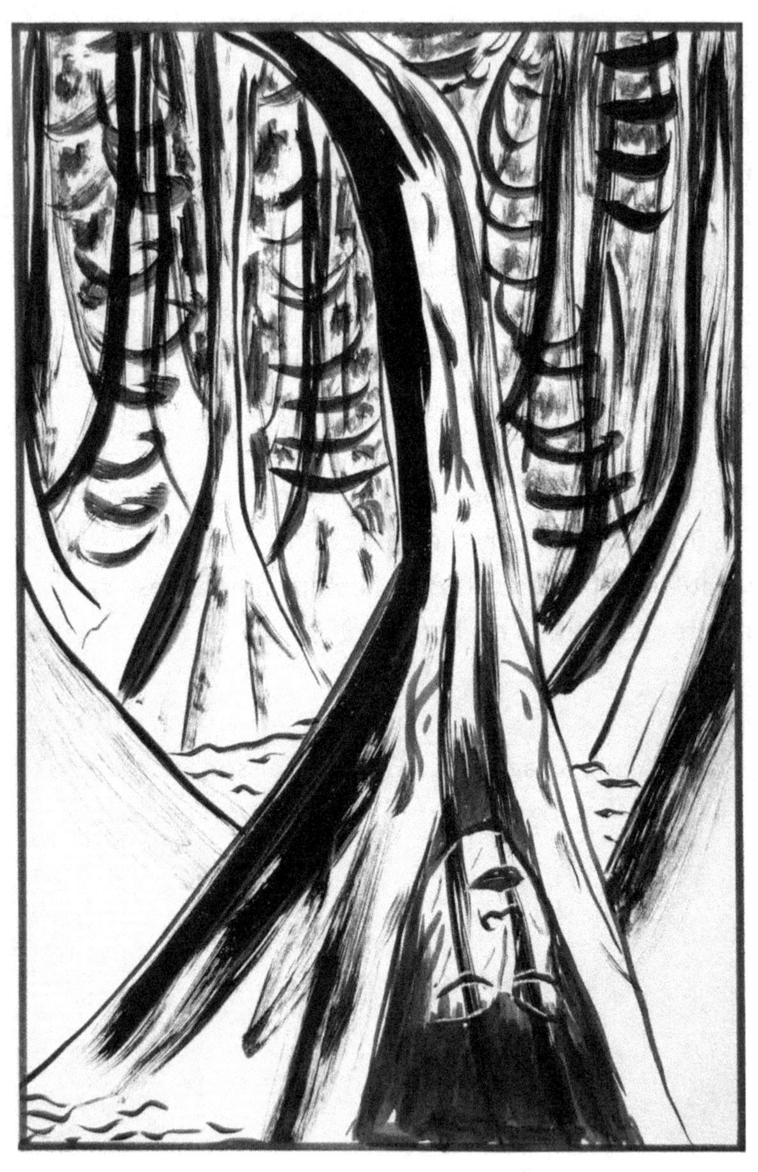

CYPRESS

The wind sweeps into the rounded clefts of her trunk, into the eye-knots of her navels. Arms braided in vines tear the sky, split into countless fingernails that claw at bruises of clouds. Her knees open over mud-stained water to ride the swelling earth. Deeper yet her feet twist through the ground, spreading and multiplying into absence.

Everything she inhales turns to blood, rushes from sky to earth, from earth to sky, driven by the beatings of a wild heart.

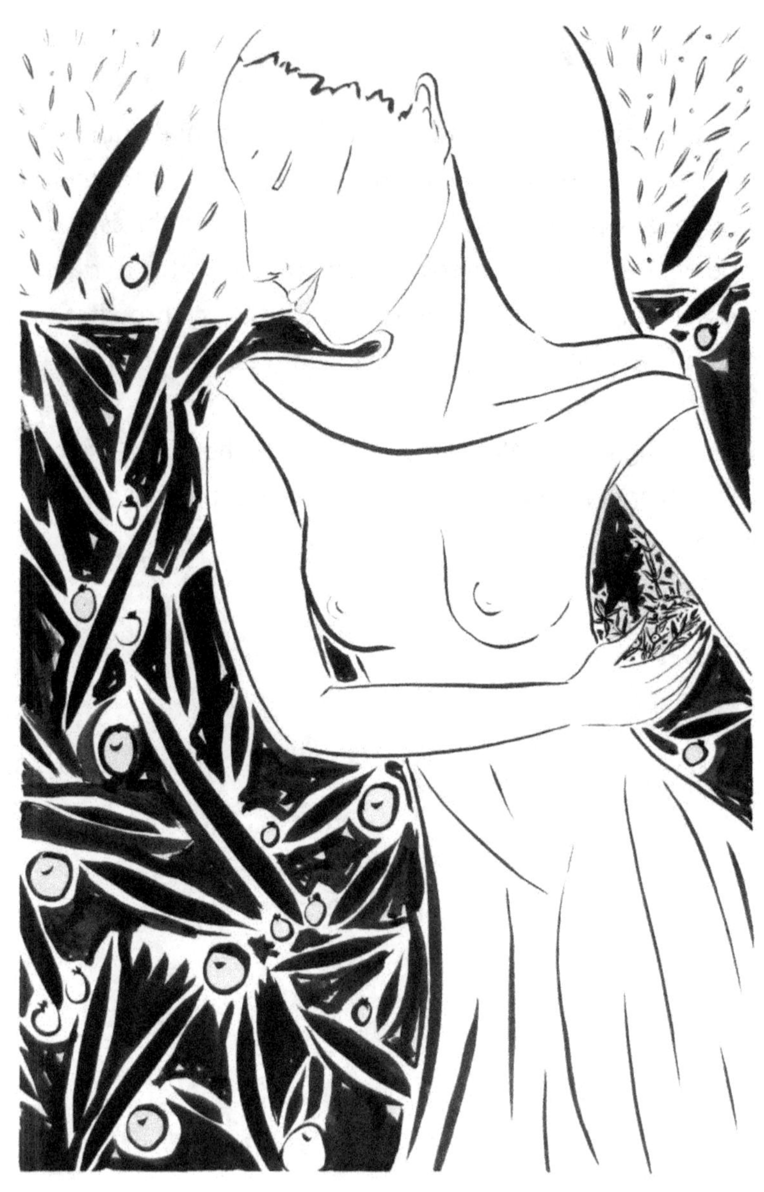

JUNIPER

I sing still green even in deepest winter. That is when I am most needed, when my berries turn blue as blood and fat as hearts. I do not mind the mouths of deer, or the hungry hands of woman or man or child who take my hearts, drink them.

Some will die of it. I do not know how to warn them.

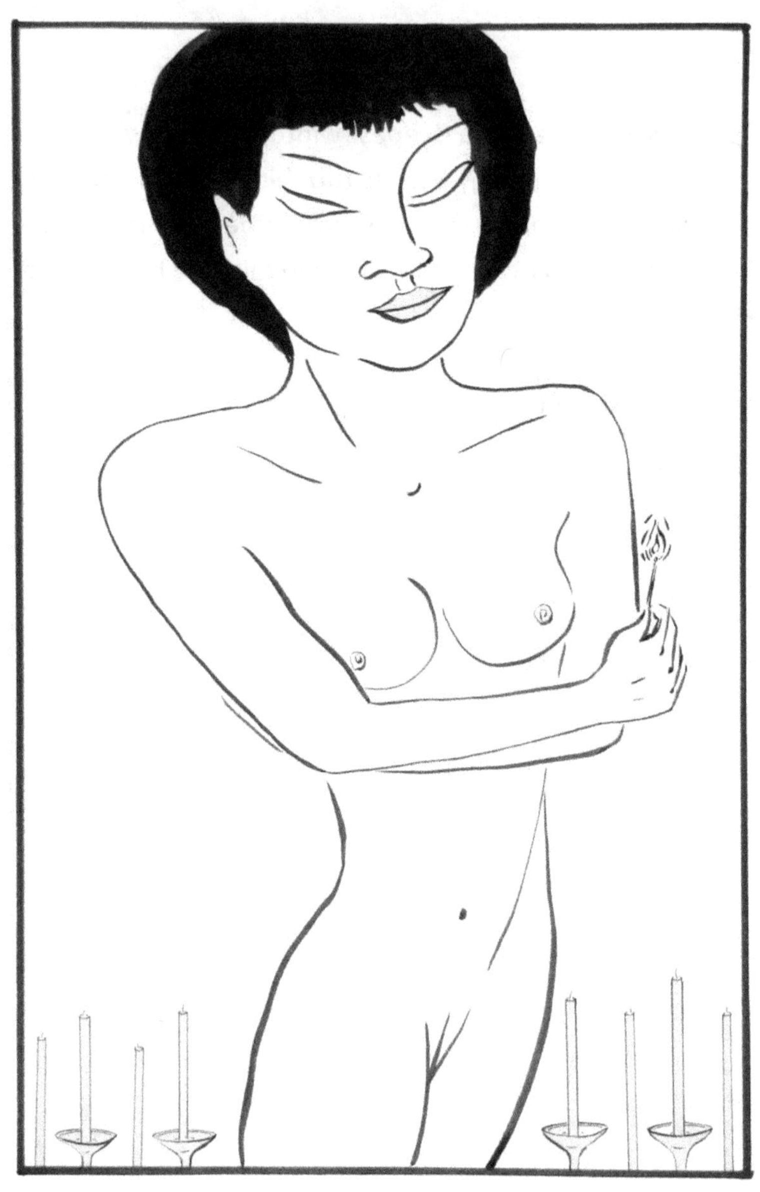

POMEGRANATE

If you could look deep enough into my wound, this is what you would see, clusters of seed-berries, fragile, holding on to each other, connected only by the white lace of my tissue. If you reached your hand inside of me, you could pluck them out, one by one. You could see through the soft, pulpy outside to the hard kernel inside. If you bit into one of them, you would be surprised at how red its juice is.

You would be surprised at how many I am.

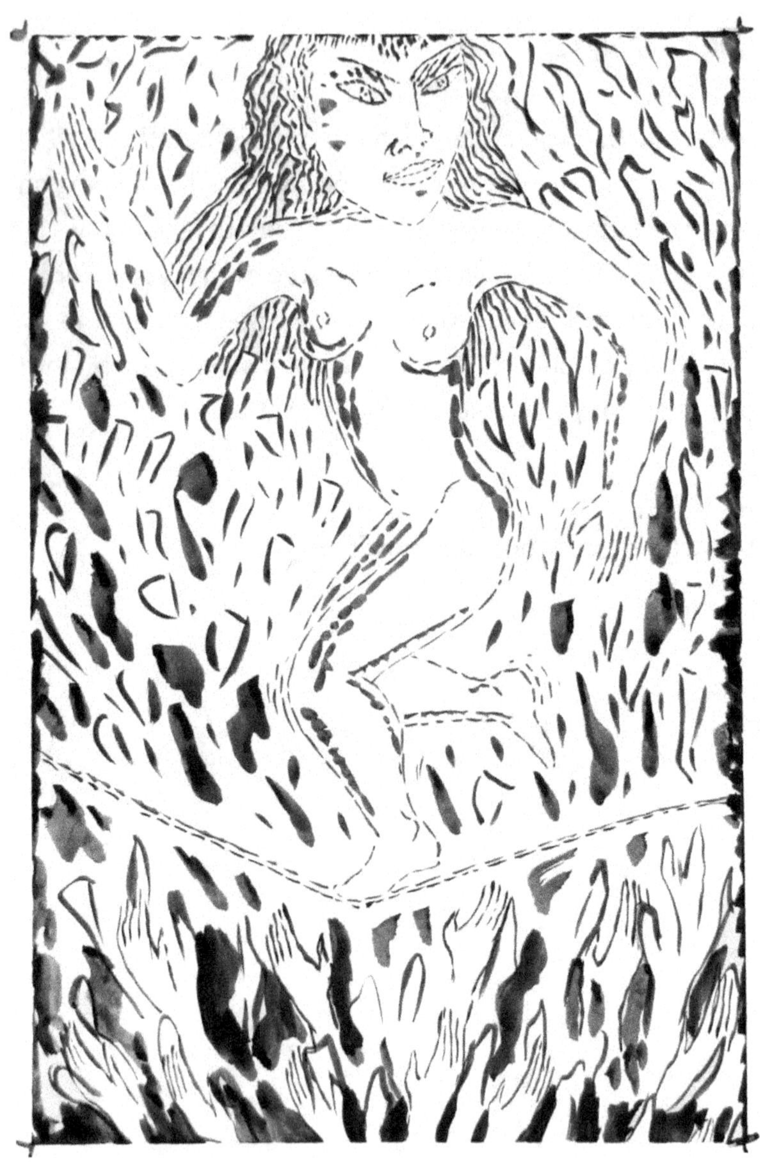

CACTUS

I am all that is milk, all that is moisture here. I am breast and vulva, I am blood of rock and sweat of desert. In times of famine they will burn my skin and feed me to their animals.

They have not learned, as my lovers have, to brave my skin.

V. Animal

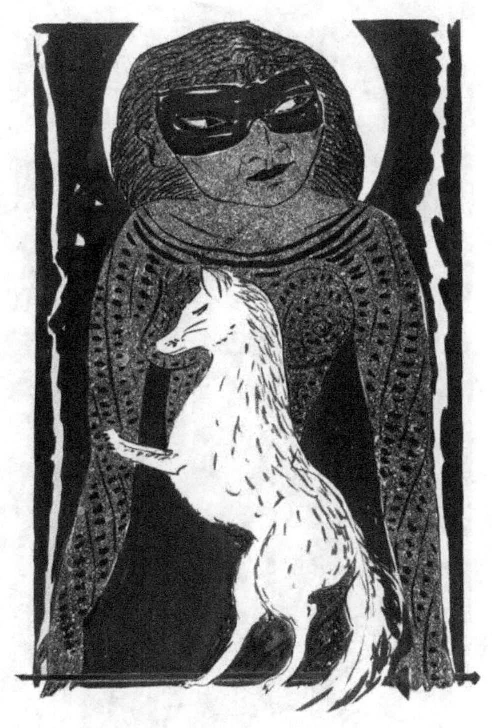

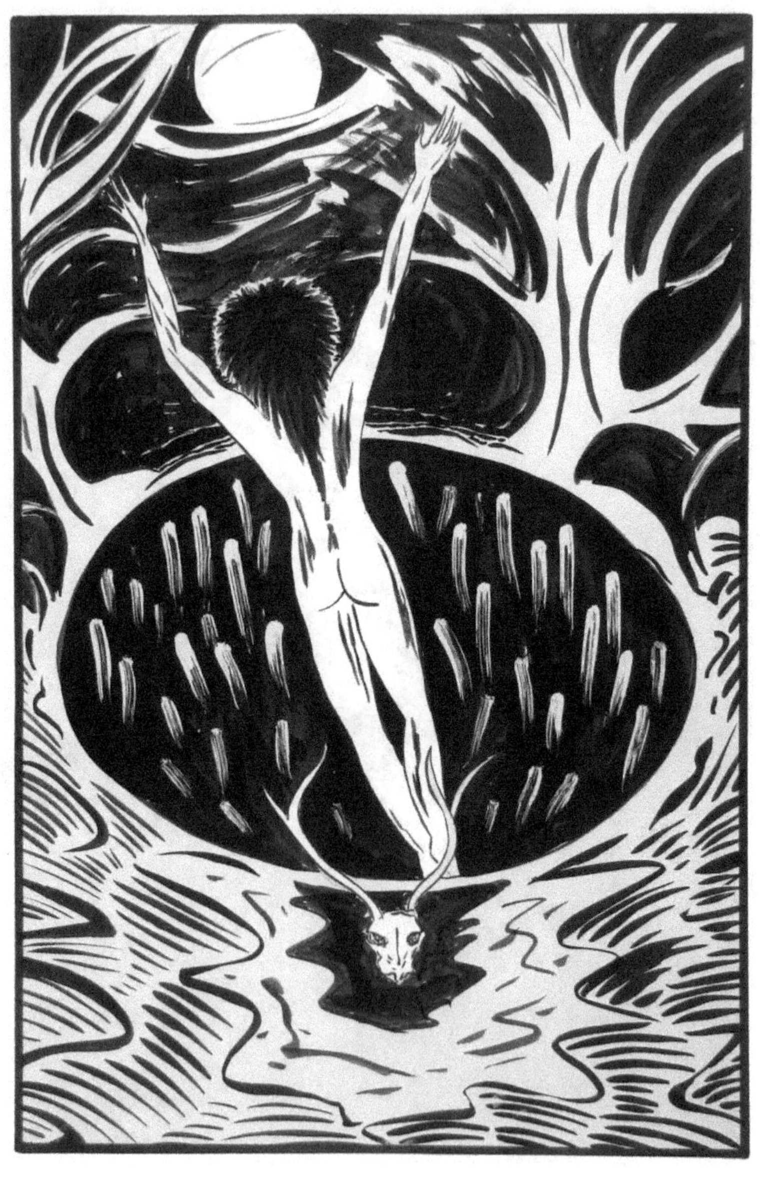

DEER

We are teachers of leaving.

You will seldom see us with the males--they leave for their own kind soon after mating. Most often we hunt with others like ourselves, mothers with young who will also leave after one season. It is the second thing we teach: first to find food, second to leave us. The first is easy and takes only a day.

The second takes our lives.

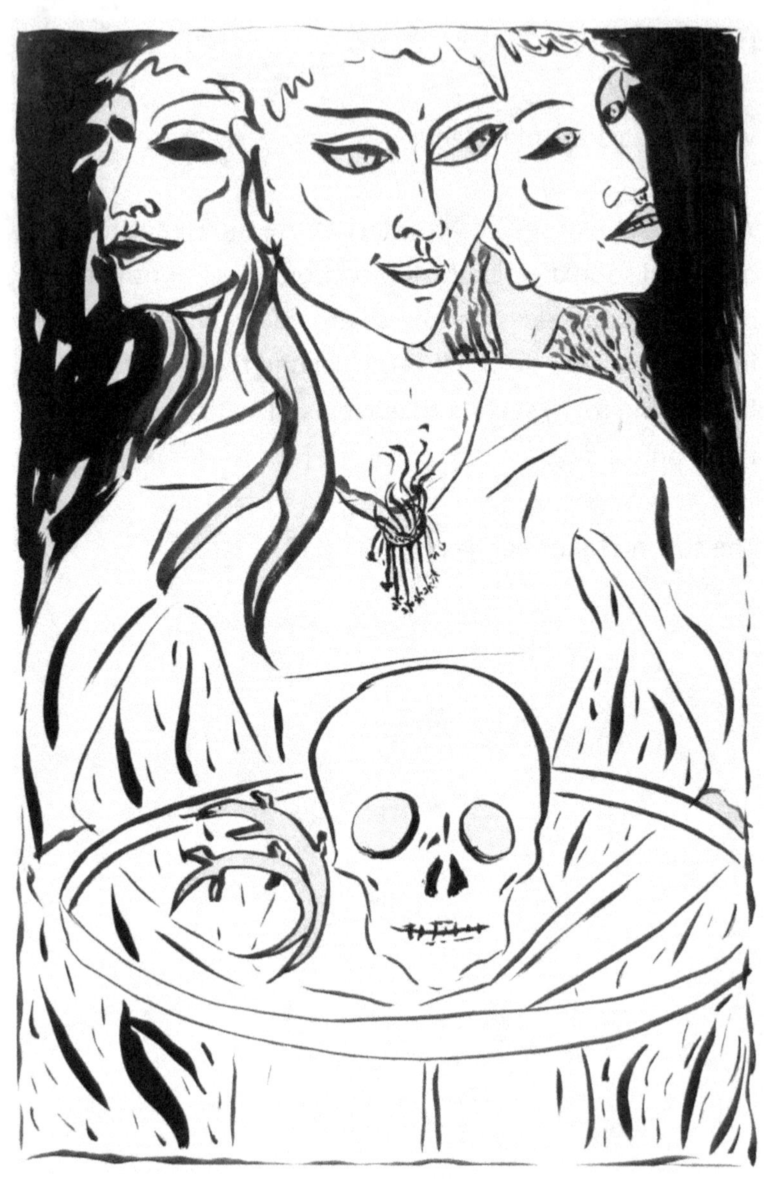

VULTURE

I am the one with a mutilated breast, I am the wounded ugly one, the roaring, the rushing, the silent. My task to wait out death.

I keep my wound hidden by soaring.

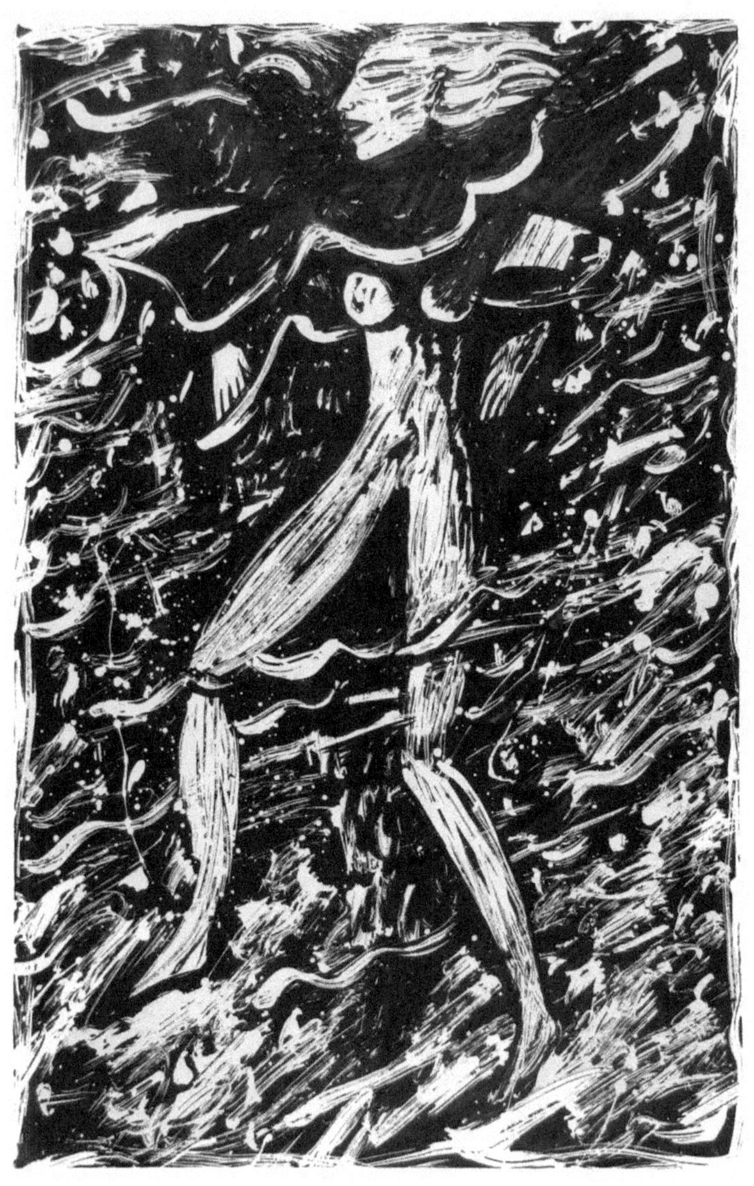

FISH

This is what she knows: that water is wise, that shadows and ripples signify death, that all nets are invisible in water.

She thinks with her body; scales and skin know if water is sweet or salt or poison.

In times of drought I have found her lying, still alive, having scooped out a womb of damp earth with her armless body, having covered herself with sand, still alive, her skin having secreted some dampness to surround her, something desperate and wet to keep her alive until spring.

VI. Human

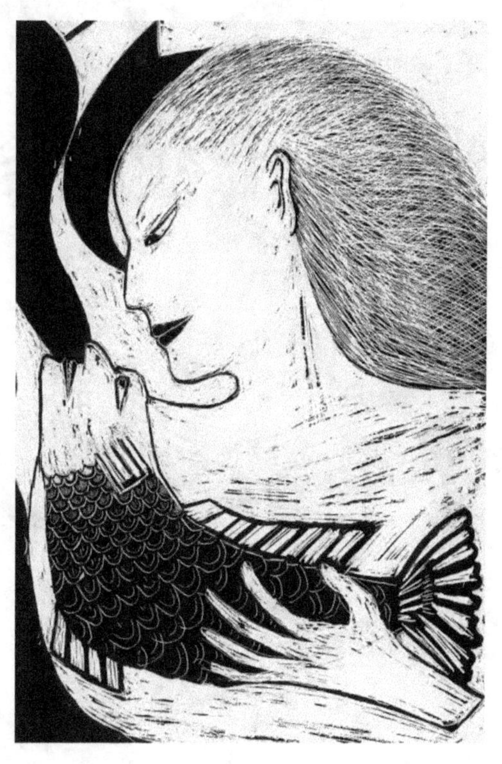

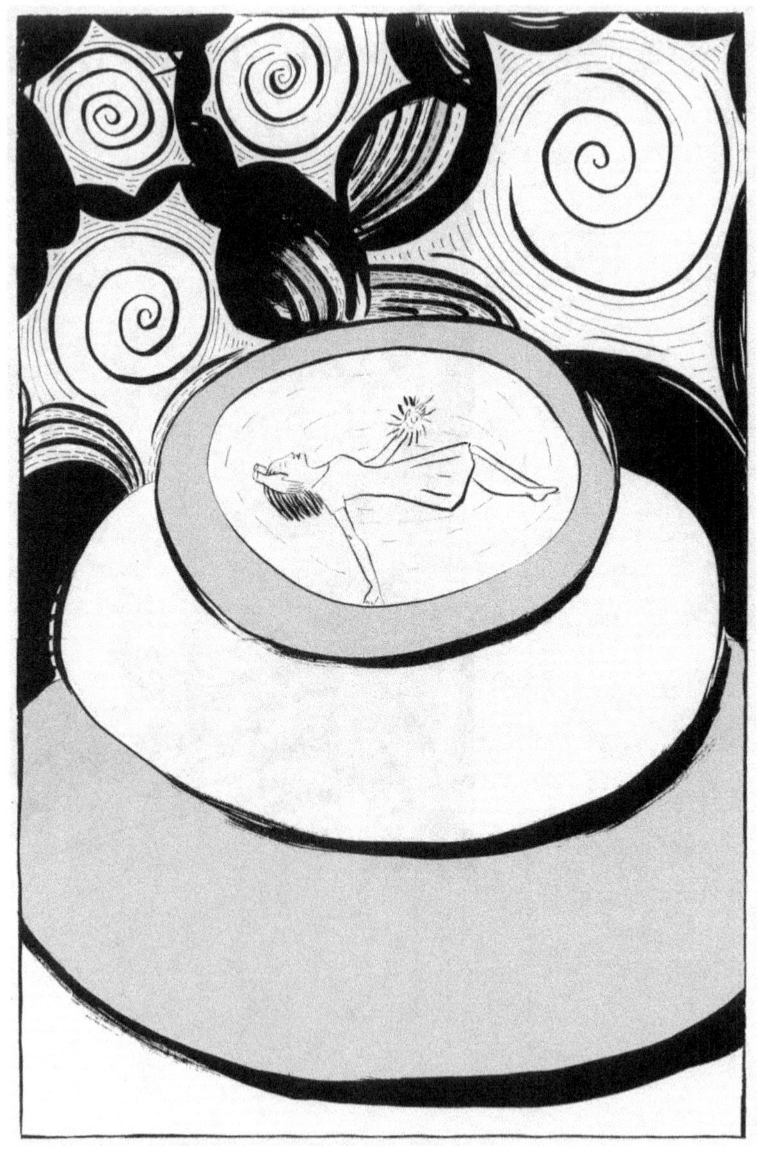

HEALER

She boils up poems in battered pots. This one for sadness. This one for loss. Here is one to help with a sick soul. She is as old as the ocean, she wears the beads of Yemaja, white and blue.

She shows me the words she spends her days gathering. How long she boils them, how she makes a syrup thick with them. She gives me a small cup of it. There is a dead bee floating on top. It tastes green, like sugar and mint, hope, the last buzzings of a bee.

Here is a bottle of poems, she says. Take a teaspoon when you feel bad.

Let me know if it works.

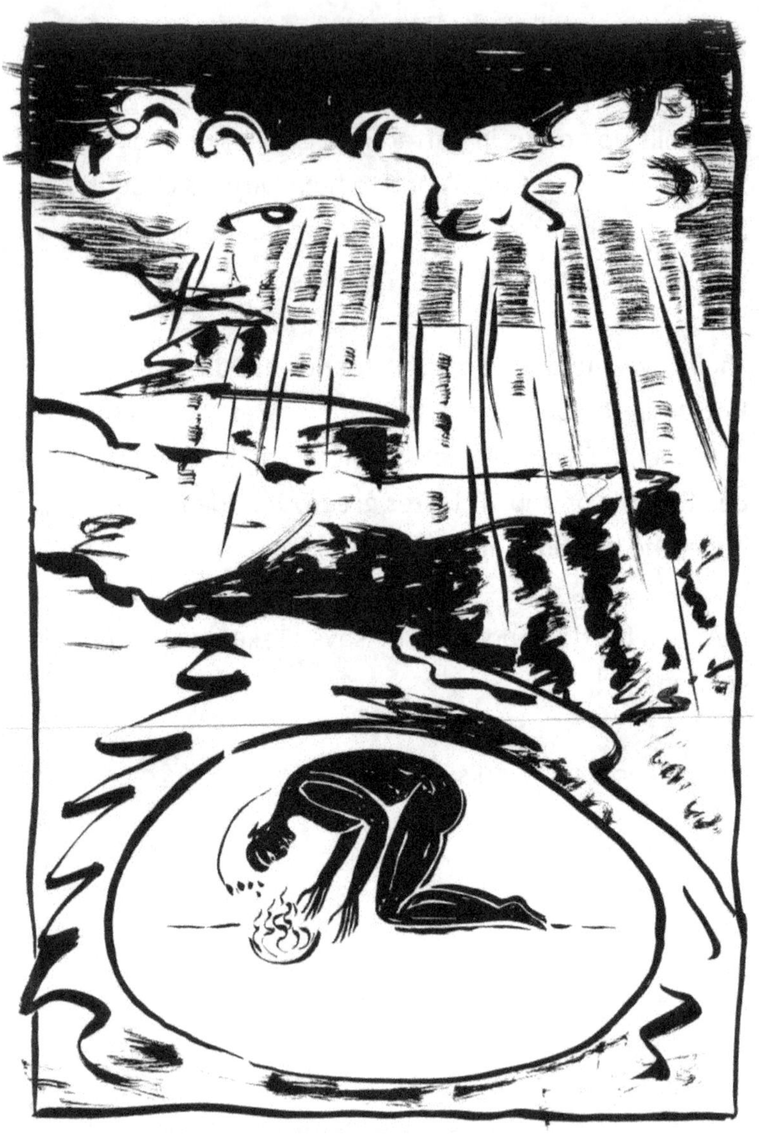

HERMIT

A hooded older woman stands in the midst of a landscape of trees and water. A cypress with Spanish moss hulks in the background and a swamp spreads out behind her. She is walking a path that leads up to the top of the mountain, although she is facing away from it. She holds a lamp that is shining brightly and her other hand is up as if pointing to the sky and a star, maybe a shooting star. Her cloak is deep green, and trimmed in gold. The swamp and trees are in her eyes. Her skin is the color of the swamp, her clothes the color of the cypress. If you could see her hair it would be the color of Spanish moss.

The swamp is the place she goes to write poems. Come with me, she says, no one is there. You won't have to speak with anyone.

You can stop pretending, she says.

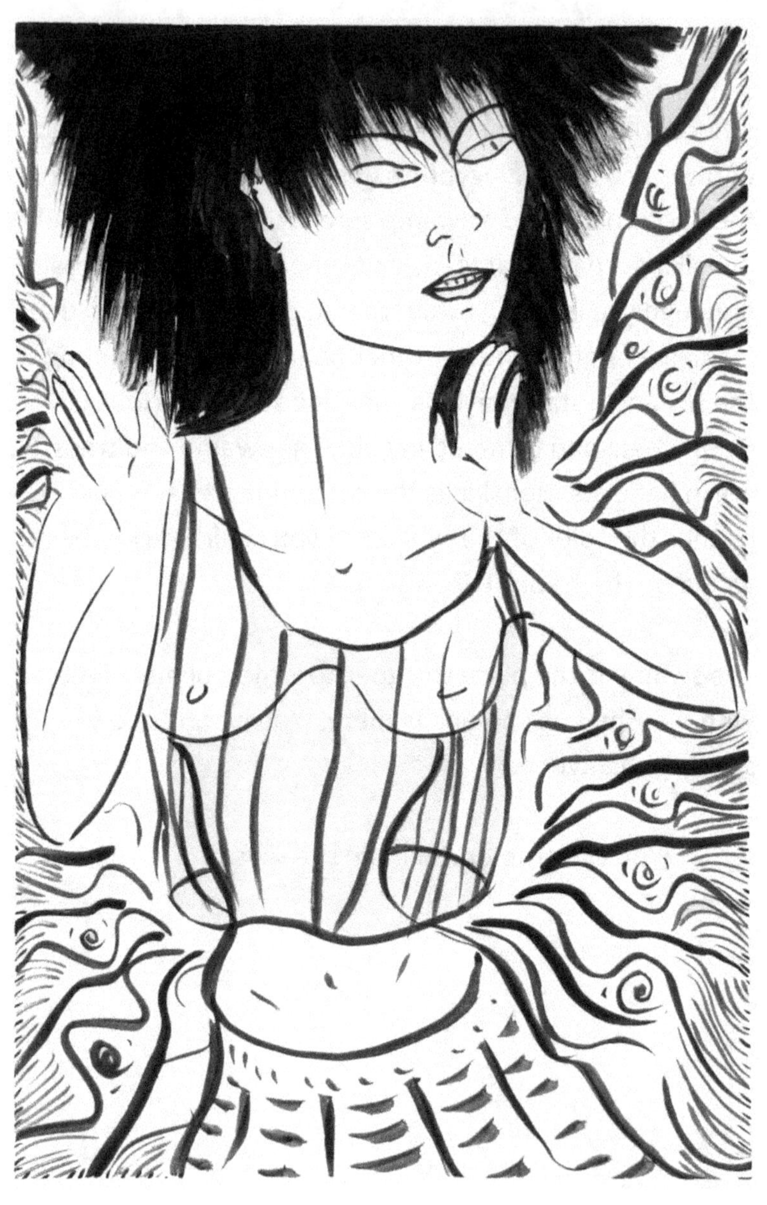

EIGHT OF SWORDS

A woman is walking through a destroyed landscape, a forest of trees and swords. Does she know that she walks through destruction? I am beginning to think she has bound and gagged herself. There are no other suspects. It is only logical. She can only move as far as her bindings will let her. There are certain things she doesn't want to see. She is so afraid she doesn't even know she is afraid.

This is what it is like to move through the world without a mother.

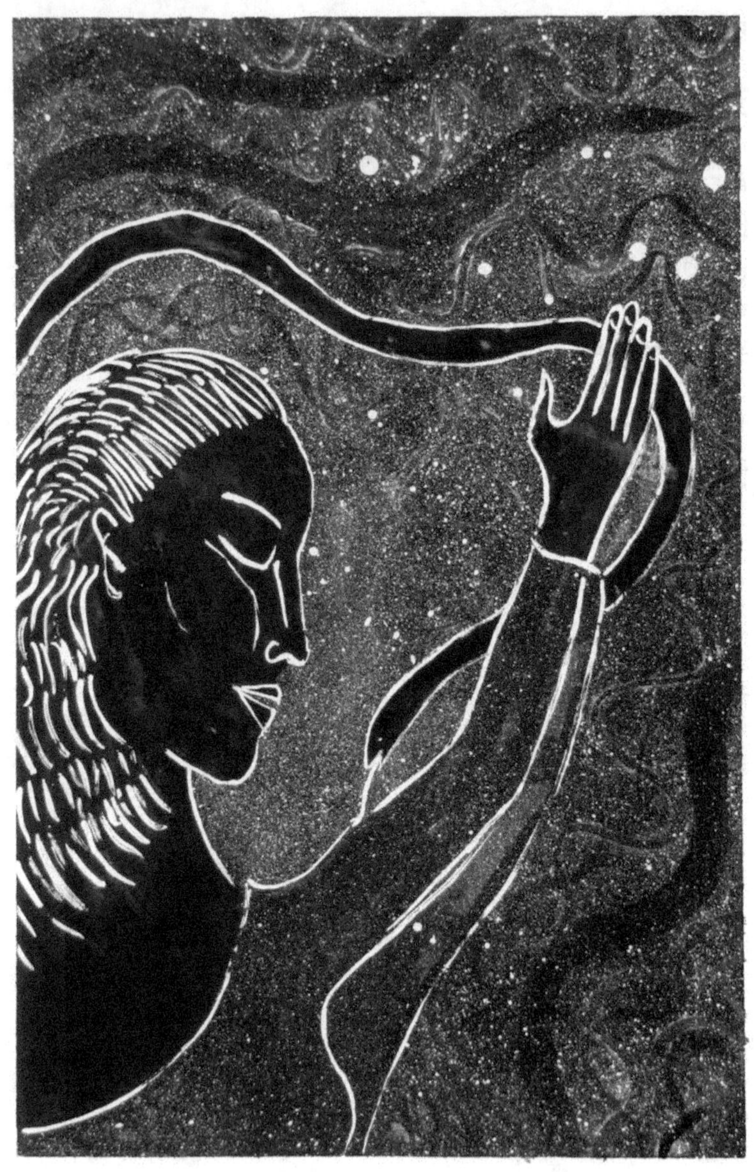

GODDESS

I search for it as I search for the demonic in me,
I look at faces of female gods with snakes and trees, see
myself in them, try to feel out where god might be in these
breasts, these nipples these hips, these lips this cunt.

AUTHOR AND ARTIST BIOS

Sheryl St. Germain

Originally from New Orleans, Sheryl St. Germain has published six poetry books, three essay collections, and co-edited two anthologies. Her latest collection of essays, *Fifty Miles,* appeared in January 2020 with Etruscan Press. She lives in Pittsburgh where she is co-founder of the Words Without Walls Program. In addition to numerous awards for her work, including two NEA grants, in 2018 she was the recipient of The Louisiana Writer Award, presented annually by the Louisiana Center for the Book. See http://sheryl-stgermain.com/ for more information.

Janet Morgan has had a long and varied art career, all with an underlying quest of depicting the energy of beings and places. Among her figurative painting series are: a pantheon of 200 deities, Wild Women, musicians and dancers (Middle Eastern and modern) and works from and about the Body's Energy. She has painted her interpretations of landscape all over the world, from Antarctica to Kyrgyzstan. She has been artist-in-residence Death Valley National Park, Weir Farm National Historic Site, the Babayan Cultural Center in Cappadocia, Turkey, Hanksville Elementary School in Utah, and the Luminous Bodies Residency at Artscape Gibraltar Point in Toronto. She has taught at the Rubin Museum of Art, the Art Students League and the Chapel of Sacred Mirrors. For 18 years she was an Expressive Arts Therapist with adult cancer patients at Sloan Ketttering. Her large paintings have been featured on stage at the Omega's Women and Power Conference in New York City, at Burning Man in Nevada and at the Parliament of World Religions in Toronto, Canada. www.janetmorgan-art.net

www.ingramcontent.com/pod-product-compliance
Lightning Source LLC
LaVergne TN
LVHW020656100826
845148LV00012B/2524

* 9 7 8 1 7 3 4 7 0 2 9 0 3 *